"For Us, The Romantic"

A collection of reflective pieces on love's complex nature; exploring family, friendship, lovers & self.

Written By
Tumi Adegoroye

Edited By
Temi Boyede

For Us, The Romantic

Copyright © 2023 Tumi Adegoroye

All rights reserved.

Paperback: 9781738807826

Electronic: 9781738807833

First Edition

Ontario, Canada

Book Cover illustrator: Katarina Naskovski

For book permissions or inquiries, please contact:

edithadegoroye@gmail.com

For Us, The Romantic

Dedication

Specially dedicated to my nephew Joshua, may you experience joy, love, peace and protection throughout your life.

This book is dedicated to people all over the world on a journey through self discovery and life's madness.

For us who are always finding ways to evolve, for us who heal through art and self reflection; may you find a way whenever you are lost, may you always know the way home.

For Us, The Romantic

Table of Contents

Glossary ix

Opening Letter xi

Lovers 1

Family & Friends 24

Self 41

For Us, The Romantic

Glossary

- Becoming

Personal Transformation

"I had focused on 'becoming' rather than just being."
— Page 49

- Being

Existing

"I had focused on becoming rather than just 'being'."
— Page 49

- On my Tod

A british slang meaning "Alone" or "by oneself."
— Page 43

For Us, The Romantic

Tumi Adegoroye

A Letter to My Readers

Dealing with love and its complexities have been a constant theme in my life. It is a journey that has driven me to madness and brought me back. But through it all, I have come to understand that love is a choice. It can be complex, but it is a beautiful thing. I define love as every feeling ever felt.

In this book, I share different aspects of my love life; how I see love through self devotion, family, friends, art, nature, people and society. The journey through love's madness can be a bumpy one, filled with highs and lows and twists and turns but it's a journey that requires patience, understanding, and a willingness to accept the imperfections of both yourself and your loved ones.

As a romantic person and a highly sensitive individual, I have found that love can be both a blessing and a hectic duty. On one hand, it allows me to feel deeply and connect with others on a level that is often hard to describe. On the other hand, it can leave me vulnerable and exposed, open to hurt and disappointment. It can make me do things I don't necessarily feel like doing, or make me act out of character.

For Us, The Romantic

But despite the challenges, I have come to realize that love is what makes life worth living. It's what gives us the strength to keep going when everything else seems to be falling apart. It is what brings us joy, happiness, and a sense of purpose.

So if you're on a journey through love's madness, know that you're not alone. We all experience the ups and downs of love, and it's okay, such is only life.

In the end, love is what makes us human. It is what gives us hope and makes life worth living. So embrace it, cherish it and never give up on it; because in the end, love is stronger than anything on earth.

These are not stories about heartbreak, but stories to help you navigate love.

I hope you enjoy this piece of work. I wish you loving days ahead and an abundance of joy.

Love, Tumi

Tumi Adegoroye

~ *Lovers* ~

For Us, The Romantic

Dear Readers,

This chapter is about the love I've experienced with my current lover and the previous lovers I've had.

Sometimes love is the best feeling that happens to us, and other times it changes its taste. Most of the time we mistake love for other feelings.

Having someone that cherishes and values you is beautiful, it's more beautiful when it's reciprocated.

Love, Tumi

Tumi Adegoroye

When our paths crossed, it felt like déjà vu
We knew each other
But not in this lifetime, in another.

It seemed as if we promised to find each other
And we did.

This love was not meant for forever
But you took it further
Even when you knew our time together was over.

So, I told you,
"I'll see you again".

Maybe in that lifetime, under these stars, it would be forever.

For Us, The Romantic

A part of me is thrilled that you are here
But it frightens me more than it excites me,
As I am haunted by love itself .
It took me on a joy ride
And left me crashing down,
Crippled with frailty and fear,
Love left the scene unharmed.
And now it's back again, to do what?
I am thrilled that you are here,
But I shall proceed with vigilance
Till the road is clear.

Lover,
Will you one day wake up to crave silence?
Grow tired of my soft kisses?
Or my naturally wide hips?
Because love had left me alone and
When I waited for years to be found,
It did not come looking for me
Nor did it drag me out of the hole.

I am thrilled that you are here.
It is scary, I must say.
So, pardon me when I am driven
By doubt and suspicion.
Let's be honest,
I called out to love again
Unsure if it would cheerfully make its way to me,
But, I seem to have fallen

Tumi Adegoroye

Into something I can't get out of.
A new hole, perhaps,
Or a trap I set my foot in.
I am unsure, and it might be too late
For me to come out of it.

But see, the love that I love might be YOU.
You carried my broken heart
And placed it back in my body.
So, believe me when I say
It frightens me more than it excites me,
But, a part of me is thrilled that you are here
Loving me.

For Us, The Romantic

I've had lovers whose love ran deep and cut me.
Wounded by obsession that I thought was love.

Tumi Adegoroye

Journal: ***Deceitful love***

I want to talk to you about something that is very close to my heart - love and its deceitfulness.

Love is a beautiful thing, but obsessing over it can be *dangerous.*

I learned this the hard way when I found myself in an earthquake of toxicity. I was in love with him, my first love, but it became an obsession. I forgot about myself and all I wanted was to love him. It wasn't until it became unbearable for my state of mind, that I made the difficult decision to leave.

It was a toxic relationship that I couldn't leave filled with heated arguments, unresolved misunderstandings, and hurtful insults. I was blinded by my obsession and so was he.

But I want to tell you that it's never too late to leave a toxic relationship. Recognize when love is good for you and when it's not.

For Us, The Romantic

Don't let your obsession blind you from the truth. Don't let the delusive charm fool you; love is not hurtful.

Love is a beautiful thing, and it is important to remember that it should never come at the cost of your own well-being.

I love you for reading this. I'm glad you are choosing yourself.

Love, Tumi

Tumi Adegoroye

    Toxicity seeps through every pore,
As I lay here, feeling unsure.
    Your touch, once sweet, now feels impure.

– Lust is not Love

For Us, The Romantic

The first burn of jealousy – feelings

- feeling fear
- feels too real
- feeling anger
- feeling guilty
- feeling bitter
- fight or flight
- feeling sadness
- feeling betrayed
- feeling threatened
- feels overwhelming
- feeling severely embarrassed

Don't let these feelings consume you.
They are normal emotions - you are human.
The way through is to be self aware, before it gets toxic.

Tumi Adegoroye

Last night in my dream
You left me
With a smile on your face
Holding hands with her
You walked away
Leaving me in a desolate place.

I woke up with tears in my eyes
Thankful it was just a dream
But my anxious mind was telling me lies
That you might leave me for real.

My one and only love
I thought the universe wouldn't dare
To come in between our core

But last night, in my dream
You left me.

I pray it won't come true
For I fear losing you
Last night in my dream
You left me.

– About Last Night

For Us, The Romantic

I feel guilty for falling in love,
As if I don't deserve it.
Walking around like this wasn't my dream,
As if my heart doesn't burst at the seams.
My friends and family think I'm proud
But really, I'm protecting my love, not loud.
I feel guilty for feeling this way,
Like I'm not allowed to love.

Why should I feel guilty for falling
When there's joy and happiness that comes with calling
Someone mine, and being theirs too?
A love that's pure, honest and true.
So, I'll shake off the guilt and embrace
The love that's come into my life with grace.
For falling in love is a beautiful thing,
And I'll cherish it with all my being.

– Guilty for falling

Tumi Adegoroye

Journal Entry: Soulmate

I wouldn't have survived the winter that year if my partner didn't support me the way he did.
It was a difficult time when even I doubted myself and thought I couldn't get out of my head. I had begun repeating mistakes, forgetting words, ignoring calls and talking to myself.

I had a partner who stayed and prayed, although there were rough nights. He kissed my face and told me it would all be fine.
He constantly reminded me of what he saw in my eyes when we first met.
He sang me songs, cooked for me and bathed me.

He said he was sure I would be back on my feet.
Even though I doubted it.
In his own words he said, "I wish you knew what you could do, you have no idea"

I melted.

I wouldn't have survived those winter months because I was confused in the brain and rugged in the heart. I trusted no one, cared very little and wanted to be all alone.

For Us, The Romantic

For the partner who loved me then, and who still sees me, hears me, loves me,
wants the best for me, supports my dreams and chases them with me: I love you dearly.

I do think we agreed to be soulmates again in this life.
I sense your spirit has loved me before, and that you were special to me.

You are still so special to me and I hope you give me the chance to cherish you the way you have worshiped me.

Love, Tums

Tumi Adegoroye

Love and hate are two strong things that can intersect, but don't allow hate in your home.

– **_Two Different Siblings_**

For Us, The Romantic

Journal: *Moody in Love*

Being in love makes me feel moody at times, as I value my private space and independence. I do occasionally wonder if I jumped into this relationship too soon; if I should have waited and played the field a little longer and learned more about myself and the world on my own.

But here I am, moody in love, trying to find a balance between being with my partner and having time to myself.

I know some may question my need for alone time, but it's important for me to recharge and strengthen myself. It doesn't mean I love my partner any less or that I'm seeking attention from others.

Love is a journey with its ups and downs, and we need to navigate through the craziness of it all. So, I ask you to understand and respect my need for time to myself. It's not a bad thing, it's a way for me to be the best partner I can be. Please understand that I do this for us, so that my sanity can remain.

Love, Tumi

Tumi Adegoroye

Now that we are in love, what now?
I ask myself this question every day
As I navigate this new terrain
With my heart on my sleeve

I thought I knew you before
As my best friend, we shared everything
But now that we are in love
I see a side of you I never knew

You're perfect in every way
Or so it seems to me
But sometimes I feel lost
Trying to be who you want me to be

We are different in many ways
But our similarities keep us together
I hope we can find a way
To navigate this new path

Now that we are in love, what now?
I don't know the answer just yet
But I'm willing to find out.

– What now

For Us, The Romantic

A Speech about Love versus Respect…

*We often find ourselves wondering which is more important in human connection: **love** or **respect**.*
We are all aware of how love is often glorified in today's world.
We are bombarded with messages and images that tell us 'love conquers all' and is the ultimate goal in a relationship.
Don't get me wrong, love is a captivating force that sweeps us off our feet and makes our heart skip a beat. It is the only beautiful thing all living things can agree on, but respect is the foundation on which love is built, it is truly the overlooked companion of love.

Any relationship can crumble under pressure if there is no respect present.
In relationships, respect allows us to truly see the other person and appreciate them. Most importantly, it allows us to acknowledge their boundaries, needs and individuality, even when it threatens 'love'.

When we prioritize respect in a relationship, we create an environment for equality and understanding. We give each other space to grow and evolve without fear of judgment or control.

*If you have respect for someone, you are able to communicate honestly and openly,
leading to solid trust.
Love is crazy because on its own it can be possessive and suffocating.
It can lead you to make decisions based only on your desires rather than considering other things and most especially, other people.*

*Respect connects our hearts and minds, helping us to build a solid foundation of mutual admiration and support.
Nurture your relationships with love and respect.*

Love conquers all, but respect helps her win the battle.

For Us, The Romantic

Whenever I see my crush, I feel excited but quite embarrassed because I become subtle, cute, nervous, pink and babyish…

    – Angelic softness

Tumi Adegoroye

"Careful, don't break"
Conversations To Handle With Love

Finding independence as a lady
Finding independence as a man
Moving in with your partner
End of a relationship
End of a friendship
Choosing a home
Race and identity
Honest criticism
Being jealous
Mental health
Saying "No"
Having kids
Illness
Abuse
Grief
Loss
Love

For Us, The Romantic

The cycle of hurting and heart break continues because of human insecurities and the fear of being vulnerable. Although, I agree that we should be cautious when falling in love, we can't truly know the heart of our next lover.
We have to walk in faith, knowing that we are here to love and so are they.
Don't be a coward; running away from love because you've been hurt.
True strength is when you have the courage to love again even when your heart has been broken a million times.

Tumi Adegoroye

Your Reflections

For Us, The Romantic

~ *Family & Friends* ~

Tumi Adegoroye

Dear Readers,

This chapter is about the love I've experienced with my family and friends.

Friendship is easy when there's understanding but it's emotionally challenging without understanding.

Love, Tums

For Us, The Romantic

You'll find that you can do it all by yourself.

                You'll realize it's easier with support.

Tumi Adegoroye

The things others dislike in you are often what your loved ones love about you.

Your laugh, your smile, your confidence, your shyness, your stubbornness…

Next time you feel small because of a stranger, think of your loved ones.

For Us, The Romantic

When I first held you, so small and new,
I couldn't describe the love I knew.
You were like an egg, fragile and pure,
And I wanted to keep you safe and secure.
As you grew, your personality shone,
A happy and brave boy, never alone.
Your smile warmed my heart and stayed
A memory that will never fade.
Playing hide and seek as you crawled,
Getting scared and excited, never stalled.
You blow me kisses through the phone,
And I know I'm not alone.
I want you to be strong,
To feed your brain berries all day long.
I pray for great days for you
And know that favor will stay true.
You bring me joy I never thought I'd find
And I love you dearly, with all my mind.
Be the best version of yourself in this life,
A smart, kind, strong, and wise man, without strife.

Love, Aunty Tumi

I will never forget the day, I almost thought I was going to lose you. You were in the hospital and in so much pain. I cried to God and told him he didn't need to bless me if that was what it would take to heal you (mind you, I know it doesn't work like that).
You had been dealing with this for years and more intensely for the last few months. It felt like, "God, where did we go wrong?", "What can we do", "What have we not done".

Mucus rolled down my nose violently and the tears came out of my eyes uncontrollably, as I cried to him, "We can't lose her!"
I know I had been out searching for friends that had no love for me, but you have been my twin, my friend and my family. So, I regret the time and years I wasted pleasing others when I should have been pleasing you.

I value you more than ever because you are my friend, my family, and you love me more than any friend could. I'm grateful to God for loving you and saving you.
I am proud of you and your body for healing itself; for doing its work. I am grateful to your organs for showing you that they don't fail. I am happy that your body is cooperating with you. I am so full of joy that you are whole.

For Us, The Romantic

Oh, I almost thought I lost you there, I will never forget the day, the pain. It will never happen. We will never see the day. We will live a peaceful life, a life of good health, a life of joy, a life of peace, filled with the promises of God.
Yes! God promised us good things and good things only are what we deserve.

I love you, and I'm glad you are here today.

– Seize each moment with your loved ones

Tumi Adegoroye

Sitting with people who
are happy knowing that
they are better than you
is like
feasting with the enemy

friends help each other
family sticks together

For Us, The Romantic

> *You might think I am the worst person on earth because of how I withdrew from the things and people I loved.*
> *I didn't want to be a silent echo, or a shadow in the dark.*
> *Unheard. Unnoticed. Unwanted. Disrespected.*

> *I left because people assumed I had a perfect life.*
> *I am starting to embrace that it is not something I can stop people from thinking;*
> *But when you think in such a manner about someone, you don't let yourself empathize with them. You can't understand them, and so you disregard their thoughts and feelings.*
> *It is toxic to stay in such environments.*

Tumi Adegoroye

We stayed friends because I saw your value
As a friend, sister, hustler, and lover, I saw your value
Even when it became unsettling, I saw your value.

I only took home the good times
You took the good, bad and ugly
You shamed my love language
And thought I was just there for the vibes.

Clearly you saw no value in me nor our friendship
You only wanted someone by your side
Not a friend you truly cherished.

For Us, The Romantic

If you are more interested in profit than the interests of others, you betray your own self.

You betray yourself when you think you've betrayed others.

Tumi Adegoroye

Dear Growing adult,

Yes, I did have a sisterhood of friends and it was beautiful; until it wasn't.
It was sweet and all I ever wanted, until it wasn't.

I can't tell you a story, but I can give you some advice.

1. *In life, surround yourself with people who see you as constantly growing (and vice-versa), so that even if you change your mind tomorrow about something, you aren't perceived as a crazy person; your friends have just discovered a fun fact about you.*
2. *Keep a no-judgment zone.*
3. *It is very important to have friends that respect you, no matter your background and experiences in life.*
4. *It is crucial to have friends that trust you - really, what's a friendship without trust.*
5. *Have friends that have an open floor for conversations, instead of friends that scare you into conversations.*
6. *Have friends that love you dearly and want you to prosper as much as they do (you should be that friend too!)*
7. *Have friends that are like sisters, so even with disagreements, love is more powerful.*

For Us, The Romantic

> 8. *Know your value, friends are good and useful in life.*
> 9. *Remember that Connections are great! But your peace of mind is greater.*
> 10. *If you have a genuine sisterhood of friendship, you should cherish it.*
> 11. *If you have 1 or 2 friends that you can call sisters, you are blessed.*

At the end of the day, surround yourself with people who understand you are the main character in your life as they are in their own lives.
You should all act accordingly and act in love.

I hope you understand.

Love, Tumi
Your favorite writing godmother

Tumi Adegoroye

Prayers and Joy

I am praying for good things to come to you. I am praying for blessings for you and yours. I am wishing you a heart and life full of joy.
I hope you get to feel what love is. I pray it stays with you.

I pray you wake up and realize you are the greatest; that the universe is you because you are God, because God lives in you.
I am praying you recognise your light and the power you have as an intelligent soul.

I hope you understand that you are brilliant in your own way, and no man can do all that you can do; because you are uniquely you.
I pray for good things to come to you. I pray you are able to discern the ungood and destroy it with the power you have. I pray you walk in your grace and glory all the days of your life. I pray you will be healthy in your soul, in your spirit and in your body all your life.

I pray you achieve all the great things you wanted to achieve on your visit to earth and beyond.

For Us, The Romantic

I pray for good news in all areas of your life.
I pray all your prayers of good come true.

Love, Tumi

Things I want for you that are possible:

- a safe life
- a gentle life
- a fun hustle
- a strong heart
- a healthy body
- a humble mind
- good character
- a peaceful soul
- fulfilled dreams
- a disciplined life
- an empathetic spirit
- a compassionate love
- a knowledgeable mind
- a beaming countenance

For Us, The Romantic

Your Reflections

Tumi Adegoroye

~ Self ~

For Us, The Romantic

Dear Readers,

Welcome to my favorite chapter where I navigate my SELF through reflections on my art, my hustle, my way of thinking and how I craft unique solutions to life challenges.

I hope you enjoy this chapter.

Love, Tumi

Tumi Adegoroye

*I have been lonely so many times that I've lost count.
It feels comfortable now,
so I don't call it loneliness anymore.
I call it, Peace .*

– *"On my tod"*

For Us, The Romantic

When you take care of yourself, you are better equipped to handle your personal and professional life.
When you take care of yourself, you are focused, present and able to give freely to others.
When you take care of yourself, you are doing the universe a favor by living in harmony with it.
It is the kind of selflessness that requires a little selfishness self-respect.
You truly have to respect yourself to understand self love.

> *– **Self respect is self love.***

Tumi Adegoroye

A core part of self love is the ability to have controlled thoughts, so that even when you are out of control, you are able to pull yourself back in and say "no".
It is the art of categorizing and letting go of unwanted thoughts that cause you anxiety.

For Us, The Romantic

Invisible Web of Self-Harm

Imposter syndrome comes in many ways and stages in our lives. Finding yourself in this invisible web of self-harm is dangerous to the psyche; here is how to come out of it:

1. **It is about your mindset:** Your thoughts become reality. For example, if you truly believe you are incapable of doing something, it would be difficult to develop the discipline to do it. So, work with your mind to think of positive possibilities.

2. **Remember it is not always about you**: You might be worried your friend thinks you are dumb, but your friend is probably worried you think the same about them, or something they are insecure about. The truth is, no one cares as much about you or your situation but you. People are busy worrying about themselves.

3. **Make courage dominant:** Fear will always come` but the secret to many things in life is taking up courage. Fear is real, but courage is dominant.

4. **Find her and feed her:** Everyone has strengths. For me, I call her, "Ms. Force". These are your talents and the things that

make you shine, the things you love about yourself, what others love about you, your good sides, your beautiful aura, your artwork, your expertise and your skills. You should find yours and feed her.

5. **Energy Up Please!:** Not only physically, but mentally too. Allow yourself to feel your feelings, but don't linger in the feeling of doubt long enough to let it break you. Embrace your highs and maintain thoughts that keep your mental energy up!

By recognizing that everyone, including the accomplished, experience moments of doubt, one can eliminate the false mask of perfection and embrace vulnerability even when we fail. Cultivating a growth mindset that values learning from failures rather than fearing them is transformative.

For Us, The Romantic

Do you sometimes feel overwhelmed by your art?
You should know that you are your art but
Your art does not always define you.

Your art is your voice,
Telling a story of a place you passed through,
Painting a picture of a journey unique to you.
It is a reflection of your soul,
Singing melodies of your passion and creativity.

Love your art because
You are your art, but remember,
Your art does not always define you.

Tumi Adegoroye

How to Fall in love With the Hustle

Hustling can be working a 'nine to five' job. It can also be owning a business or being a manager, doctor, stripper, tailor, hawker, designer, rapper, analyst, cleaner, cook and the list goes on.
All work is a hustle.

I fell in love with hustling when I repeated a class in high school. I had to re-do that class again. The whole year. I learnt how to be resourceful on my own. I truly learnt that in life everything is pretty much an exam. Getting good grades, being a tidy human, being a responsible person, being obedient - we learn, we fail, then we realize, "Oh, that was wrong, this is how it should be done, I see". After repeating the class, I re-learnt how to read, study, talk, walk, dress and act.

I pivoted.
I became a top grader because I had focused on "becoming" rather than just "being" by doing three things. The first, being: ***coming to the realization of my unwillingness to learn.*** I disliked exams and everything being taught in school. All I wanted was a free day and some sleep.
After failing a class and understanding I was going to

experience a year with my friends moving on without me, I felt shame. I came to accept it, but I needed to pass this next year. How was that going to happen?

Understanding I had no interest in school, I forced myself to have an interest in the context of what was being taught.
I simply now "wanted to know" for my sake of personal knowledge, so I adapted a belief to drive my enthusiasm.

My solution was to **"get excited"**. This was the second thing that sealed my love for "becoming".

Being excited means you are happy to do something, and most of the time if humans don't like a thing, we will not get excited about it.
I decided to force myself to get excited because I believed if I had the right resources to pass this exam, I could do it.
This is the internal conversation I had with myself:
"I have my brain working well. My hands, my ears, all my organs are good, yes? I might be worried over a boy, but am I that heart broken? My heart still works, right? I am beautiful and I am alive, right? I was able to get to this stage just doing and being me, right? Okay, Tumi, let's be happy. Let's get excited

that we are about to do this and it will be successful. I can't wait for the results, imagine the amazing results. This will be great, let's go!".

I still have this conversation with myself over and over again everyday, so about 5 times a day and 5 times a week. I adopted this thought when I was only 12, and each time I felt like I needed to do something big like a hustle or to put out a project that felt like too much work, I would talk to myself in this way. It is a superpower we all have but forget to use.
It's called: The art of Gratitude.

Life is good when you have all the things you need to hustle. Life is more exciting when you have all you need to chase your dreams and so the third thing I did was to **develop a healthy mental and physical state**. Being physically and mentally well gives you a high chance of succeeding when you get a big opportunity.

This is how I fell in love with hard work.

I do have my days, but this is how I snap back and get back in the game.
Exciting, isn't it?

For Us, The Romantic

I came to understand that if you don't pass a stage, you don't move on to the next level - and this applies to every stage in life, not only school.
Even after one passes a stage, it might not be to their satisfaction. So, they go back to the board and do things a little differently to achieve a better result. No matter the stage you're at or hustle you're in, adopting a certain mindset can shift your trajectory.

Tumi Adegoroye

Be honest about who you are loving.
Are you doing yourself a disservice?

You can try your best to heal from dusk till dawn, but you won't heal if you don't come to terms with who you are loving.
If you never accept who they have been to you, it will be hard to let go of the trauma.

Be honest with who you are loving and love yourself enough to walk away if you are doing yourself a disservice.

Who told you self love was all fun?

For Us, The Romantic

She traveled far to find
something that could
help her and her tribe.
earth's real gold.

She met him thinking,
"he will lead me there"
and truly he did.
he took her with
nothing to spare.

She traveled far and found
that this was no cure.
it was a dazzling display
of nature's tricks.

On a tree branch,
she found words written,
waiting to be spoken.
affirmations and prayers
formed to be brought to life.

How could this be the cure?
words with layers of
wisdom and prayers for heirs.

She returned home after
she traveled far to find
something that could
help her and her tribe.

Tumi Adegoroye

She sat with the words and spoke
and was bathed in God's eternal light
Bringing life to her.

Reborn
she feels whole and understands
she is her own treasure
a golden rebirth
born anew from the words she found.

Those words were hers
written when she was young
with a pure and innocent face.

The people found that
they were God's heir
the golden children
the joy of rainbows
the warriors of the forests
the favored beings.

There is strength in suffering,
but the power of the mouth
changes dimensions and embraces
precious realities to come

> **– *When you're lost, speak powerful words***

For Us, The Romantic

It's very difficult having relationships when you find solace in solitude.
You shouldn't feel guilty for wanting time to yourself.
I've always felt like I could think better, breathe better and do things better when I'm alone because I have no distractions.
It feels as though I can function properly when I'm in my space.
You can be alone, and not lonely.
It's when you're alone you are able to master yourself, hear your voice and act according to your dreams.
Embrace knowing yourself and loving yourself in solitude.

Tumi Adegoroye

healing
from
anything
is
a
task
only
you
can
truly
carry
out.

For Us, The Romantic

Sometimes we are blinded by the lives of others,
wondering what life would be like in their shoes;
wanting to wear their skin and live their bright lives.

We should let go of envy and release it into the night.
We are meant to be free just like love.
Free and content with what we have and who we are.

Tumi Adegoroye

You don't have to be perfect to take pictures.
You don't have to be perfect to post on your feed.
There shouldn't have be perfection in creating memories,
having a good time, or being yourself.

For Us, The Romantic

Healing alone offers a space for self discovery, however it has its pros and cons.

When healing alone, you can allow yourself to build a sense of self-reliance and independence without the distraction of people. You are able to dedicate time to your personal growth and better navigate your emotions while learning about yourself.

On the other side of the coin, you might have a limited perspective, and with a limited perspective, you lack a broad understanding of life. Healing alone can also lead to loneliness and isolation due to lack of social support.

Pick a pill; or take both.

Tumi Adegoroye

When someone says life is good,
They are happy,
They are where they are meant to be,
Things are moving around them,
They are at peace.

They are living the dreams they've dreamt,
Prayers they've prayed,
Conversations they've had.

They have the things they need to chase their dreams.
Their loved ones are at peace.
Life is good because they have all they need to
succeed.

For Us, The Romantic

Making time and space to daydream is part of creating the life you wish for.
Drafting a plan is organizing your steps.
Taking action on it is manifesting it physically.
Completing the action is bringing it to life completely.

This is how you manifest what you've wished for:

Dreaming + Planning + Doing = Answered prayers

Tumi Adegoroye

Reflections - Art Me

I write my feelings, so I can understand them.
I write my thoughts, so I can learn from my actions.
I write for my soul, so I can reflect and grow.
I write openly for people who experience what I do, so they are aware that they are not alone.
I show my strength but people think I'm looking for attention.
I create art from my feelings and people think, "*who does she think she is*".

Oh well! I have found joy in doing what I want, because these pieces are for me and *my* generations - for them to learn about life, love, growing and most importantly: Me.

I am not hiding my face anymore.
I am not burying my art even if it makes you uncomfortable.
I love my art and I love the joy it brings me.
I am leaving my mark on the world.
I am leaving my mark on my generations.
It's too late for those who think it's irrelevant.
My fingerprint is all over the digital realm.
I have left my mark all over its face.
I am who I am and my art is what it is - me.

I am here and I always will be.

For Us, The Romantic

I am my own healer,
I soothe my body and soul.

I am my own maker,
I create the life I want.

I am my own boss,
I get things done.

I am my own lover,
I show myself kindness and affection.

I am my own leader,
I lead the way and allow myself to be led.

I am all I want to be
I will be all I aim to be
As God is in me.

Tumi Adegoroye

Your Reflections

For Us, The Romantic

AFFIRMATIONS

I find affirmations powerful, that even when I'm not in the right state of mind to speak these words, I do and they work.

It's a prayer guide for me - It works because I believe what I say.

Repeat:

I have everything I need to create the life I want.

I am healthy and my body will constantly heal itself.

I am loved because my creator loved me first so, I will share love too.

I am blessed because all the blessings of God are mine.

I know my future is great, it will forever shine.

I will give to others because I have in abundance.

I am happy because it is well with all of me.

Tumi Adegoroye

END NOTE

I am romantic with my family
I am romantic with my friends
I am romantic with my partner
I am romantic with myself
It is hearty, affectionate, passionate and filled with so much warmth.

I have a desire to be with you.
To love you and cherish you is my way of being with you.
It is my lifestyle.

I love you.

For Us, The Romantic

Special thanks to my lover, my sister, my best friend and my cousin.

Thanks for your support while publishing this book.

Special thanks to my editor Temi Boyede for coming on this journey with me.

Special thanks to my readers for your support.

www.ingramcontent.com/pod-product-compliance
Lightning Source LLC
Chambersburg PA
CBHW021130080526
44587CB00012B/1220